Sophocles

Oedipus Rex

Translated by F. Storr (1912)

OEDIPUS REX

ARGUMENT

To Laius, King of Thebes, an oracle foretold that the child born to him by his queen Jocasta would slay his father and wed his mother. So when in time a son was born the infant's feet were riveted together and he was left to die on Mount Cithaeron. But a shepherd found the babe and tended him, and delivered him to another shepherd who took him to his master, the King of Corinth. Polybus being childless adopted the boy, who grew up believing that he was indeed the King's son. Afterwards doubting his parentage he inquired of the Delphic god and heard himself the word declared before to Laius. Wherefore he fled from what he deemed his father's house and in his flight he encountered and unwillingly slew his father Laius. Arriving at Thebes he answered the riddle of the Sphinx and the grateful Thebans made their deliverer king. So he reigned in the room of Laius, and espoused the widowed queen. Children were born to them and Thebes prospered under his rule, but again a grievous plague fell upon the city. Again the oracle was consulted and it bade them purge themselves of blood-guiltiness. Oedipus denounces the crime of which he is unaware, and undertakes to track out the criminal. Step by step it is brought home to him that he is the man. The closing scene reveals Jocasta slain by her own hand and Oedipus blinded by his own act and praying for death or exile.

DRAMATIS PERSONAE

Oedipus.
The Priest of Zeus.
Creon.
Chorus of Theban Elders.

Teiresias.
Jocasta.
Messenger.
Herd of Laius.
Second Messenger.

Scene: Thebes. Before the Palace of Oedipus.

OEDIPUS THE KING

Suppliants of all ages are seated round the altar at the palace doors,
at their head a PRIEST OF ZEUS. To them enter OEDIPUS.

OEDIPUS
My children, latest born to Cadmus old,
Why sit ye here as suppliants, in your hands
Branches of olive filleted with wool?
What means this reek of incense everywhere,
And everywhere laments and litanies?
Children, it were not meet that I should learn
From others, and am hither come, myself,
I Oedipus, your world-renowned king.
Ho! aged sire, whose venerable locks
Proclaim thee spokesman of this company,
Explain your mood and purport. Is it dread
Of ill that moves you or a boon ye crave?
My zeal in your behalf ye cannot doubt;
Ruthless indeed were I and obdurate
If such petitioners as you I spurned.

PRIEST
Yea, Oedipus, my sovereign lord and king,
Thou seest how both extremes of age besiege
Thy palace altars—fledglings hardly winged,
and greybeards bowed with years; priests, as am I
of Zeus, and these the flower of our youth.
Meanwhile, the common folk, with wreathed boughs
Crowd our two market-places, or before
Both shrines of Pallas congregate, or where
Ismenus gives his oracles by fire.
For, as thou seest thyself, our ship of State,
Sore buffeted, can no more lift her head,
Foundered beneath a weltering surge of blood.
A blight is on our harvest in the ear,
A blight upon the grazing flocks and herds,
A blight on wives in travail; and withal
Armed with his blazing torch the God of Plague
Hath swooped upon our city emptying
The house of Cadmus, and the murky realm
Of Pluto is full fed with groans and tears.

Therefore, O King, here at thy hearth we sit,
I and these children; not as deeming thee
A new divinity, but the first of men;
First in the common accidents of life,
And first in visitations of the Gods.
Art thou not he who coming to the town   40
of Cadmus freed us from the tax we paid
To the fell songstress? Nor hadst thou received
Prompting from us or been by others schooled;
No, by a god inspired (so all men deem,
And testify) didst thou renew our life.
And now, O Oedipus, our peerless king,
All we thy votaries beseech thee, find
Some succor, whether by a voice from heaven
Whispered, or haply known by human wit.
Tried counselors, methinks, are aptest found 1   50
To furnish for the future pregnant rede.
Upraise, O chief of men, upraise our State!
Look to thy laurels! for thy zeal of yore
Our country's savior thou art justly hailed:
O never may we thus record thy reign:—
"He raised us up only to cast us down."
Uplift us, build our city on a rock.
Thy happy star ascendant brought us luck,
O let it not decline! If thou wouldst rule
This land, as now thou reignest, better sure   60
To rule a peopled than a desert realm.
Nor battlements nor galleys aught avail,
If men to man and guards to guard them tail.

OEDIPUS
Ah! my poor children, known, ah, known too well,
The quest that brings you hither and your need.
Ye sicken all, well wot I, yet my pain,
How great soever yours, outtops it all.
Your sorrow touches each man severally,
Him and none other, but I grieve at once
Both for the general and myself and you.   70
Therefore ye rouse no sluggard from day-dreams.
Many, my children, are the tears I've wept,
And threaded many a maze of weary thought.
Thus pondering one clue of hope I caught,
And tracked it up; I have sent Menoeceus' son,

Creon, my consort's brother, to inquire
Of Pythian Phoebus at his Delphic shrine,
How I might save the State by act or word.
And now I reckon up the tale of days
Since he set forth, and marvel how he fares.   80
'Tis strange, this endless tarrying, passing strange.
But when he comes, then I were base indeed,
If I perform not all the god declares.

PRIEST
Thy words are well timed; even as thou speakest
That shouting tells me Creon is at hand.

OEDIPUS
O King Apollo! may his joyous looks
Be presage of the joyous news he brings!

PRIEST
As I surmise, 'tis welcome; else his head
Had scarce been crowned with berry-laden bays.

OEDIPUS
We soon shall know; he's now in earshot range.   90
[Enter CREON]
My royal cousin, say, Menoeceus' child,
What message hast thou brought us from the god?

CREON
Good news, for e'en intolerable ills,
Finding right issue, tend to naught but good.

OEDIPUS
How runs the oracle? thus far thy words
Give me no ground for confidence or fear.

CREON
If thou wouldst hear my message publicly,
I'll tell thee straight, or with thee pass within.

OEDIPUS
Speak before all; the burden that I bear
Is more for these my subjects than myself.   100

CREON

Let me report then all the god declared.
King Phoebus bids us straitly extirpate
A fell pollution that infests the land,
And no more harbor an inveterate sore.

OEDIPUS

What expiation means he? What's amiss?

CREON

Banishment, or the shedding blood for blood.
This stain of blood makes shipwreck of our state.

OEDIPUS

Whom can he mean, the miscreant thus denounced?

CREON

Before thou didst assume the helm of State,
The sovereign of this land was Laius.

OEDIPUS

I heard as much, but never saw the man.

CREON

He fell; and now the god's command is plain:
Punish his takers-off, whoe'er they be.

OEDIPUS

Where are they? Where in the wide world to find
The far, faint traces of a bygone crime?

CREON

In this land, said the god; "who seeks shall find;
Who sits with folded hands or sleeps is blind."

OEDIPUS

Was he within his palace, or afield,
Or traveling, when Laius met his fate?

CREON

Abroad; he started, so he told us, bound
For Delphi, but he never thence returned.

OEDIPUS

Came there no news, no fellow-traveler
To give some clue that might be followed up?

CREON
But one escape, who flying for dear life,
Could tell of all he saw but one thing sure.

OEDIPUS
And what was that? One clue might lead us far,
With but a spark of hope to guide our quest.

CREON
Robbers, he told us, not one bandit but
A troop of knaves, attacked and murdered him.

OEDIPUS
Did any bandit dare so bold a stroke,
Unless indeed he were suborned from Thebes? 130

CREON
So 'twas surmised, but none was found to avenge
His murder mid the trouble that ensued.

OEDIPUS
What trouble can have hindered a full quest,
When royalty had fallen thus miserably?

CREON
The riddling Sphinx compelled us to let slide
The dim past and attend to instant needs.

OEDIPUS
Well, I will start afresh and once again
Make dark things clear. Right worthy the concern
Of Phoebus, worthy thine too, for the dead;
I also, as is meet, will lend my aid   140
To avenge this wrong to Thebes and to the god.
Not for some far-off kinsman, but myself,
Shall I expel this poison in the blood;
For whoso slew that king might have a mind
To strike me too with his assassin hand.
Therefore in righting him I serve myself.
Up, children, haste ye, quit these altar stairs,

Take hence your suppliant wands, go summon hither
The Theban commons. With the god's good help
Success is sure; 'tis ruin if we fail.   150
[Exeunt OEDIPUS and CREON]

PRIEST
Come, children, let us hence; these gracious words
Forestall the very purpose of our suit.
And may the god who sent this oracle
Save us withal and rid us of this pest.
[Exeunt PRIEST and SUPPLIANTS]

CHORUS
(Str. 1)
Sweet-voiced daughter of Zeus from thy gold-paved
Pythian shrine
        Wafted to Thebes divine,
What dost thou bring me? My soul is racked and shivers
with fear.
        (Healer of Delos, hear!)
Hast thou some pain unknown before,   160
Or with the circling years renewest a penance of yore?
Offspring of golden Hope, thou voice immortal, O tell
me.

(Ant. 1)
First on Athene I call; O Zeus-born goddess, defend!
        Goddess and sister, befriend,
Artemis, Lady of Thebes, high-throned in the midst of
our mart!
        Lord of the death-winged dart!
        Your threefold aid I crave
        From death and ruin our city to save.   170
If in the days of old when we nigh had perished, ye drave
From our land the fiery plague, be near us now and
defend us!

(Str. 2)
        Ah me, what countless woes are mine!
        All our host is in decline;
        Weaponless my spirit lies.
        Earth her gracious fruits denies;
        Women wail in barren throes;

Life on life downstriken goes,
Swifter than the wind bird's flight,
Swifter than the Fire-God's might,
To the westering shores of Night.

(Ant. 2)
    Wasted thus by death on death
    All our city perisheth.
    Corpses spread infection round;
    None to tend or mourn is found.
    Wailing on the altar stair
    Wives and grandams rend the air—
    Long-drawn moans and piercing cries
    Blent with prayers and litanies.
    Golden child of Zeus, O hear
    Let thine angel face appear!

(Str. 3)
And grant that Ares whose hot breath I feel,
    Though without targe or steel
He stalks, whose voice is as the battle shout,
May turn in sudden rout,
To the unharbored Thracian waters sped,
    Or Amphitrite's bed.
    For what night leaves undone,
    Smit by the morrow's sun
Perisheth. Father Zeus, whose hand
Doth wield the lightning brand,
Slay him beneath thy levin bold, we pray,
    Slay him, O slay!

(Ant. 3)
O that thine arrows too, Lycean King,
    From that taut bow's gold string,
Might fly abroad, the champions of our rights;
    Yea, and the flashing lights
Of Artemis, wherewith the huntress sweeps
    Across the Lycian steeps.
Thee too I call with golden-snooded hair,
    Whose name our land doth bear,
Bacchus to whom thy Maenads Evoe shout;
    Come with thy bright torch, rout,
    Blithe god whom we adore,

180

190

200

210

The god whom gods abhor.

[Enter OEDIPUS.]
OEDIPUS
Ye pray; 'tis well, but would ye hear my words
And heed them and apply the remedy,
Ye might perchance find comfort and relief.
Mind you, I speak as one who comes a stranger   2 20
To this report, no less than to the crime;
For how unaided could I track it far
Without a clue? Which lacking (for too late
Was I enrolled a citizen of Thebes)
This proclamation I address to all:—
Thebans, if any knows the man by whom
Laius, son of Labdacus, was slain,
I summon him to make clean shrift to me.
And if he shrinks, let him reflect that thus
Confessing he shall 'scape the capital charge;   2 30
For the worst penalty that shall befall him
Is banishment—unscathed he shall depart.
But if an alien from a foreign land
Be known to any as the murderer,
Let him who knows speak out, and he shall have
Due recompense from me and thanks to boot.
But if ye still keep silence, if through fear
For self or friends ye disregard my hest,
Hear what I then resolve; I lay my ban
On the assassin whosoe'er he be.
Let no man in this land, whereof I hold   2 40
The sovereign rule, harbor or speak to him;
Give him no part in prayer or sacrifice
Or lustral rites, but hound him from your homes.
For this is our defilement, so the god
Hath lately shown to me by oracles.
Thus as their champion I maintain the cause
Both of the god and of the murdered King.
And on the murderer this curse I lay
(On him and all the partners in his guilt):—
Wretch, may he pine in utter wretchedness!   2 50
And for myself, if with my privity
He gain admittance to my hearth, I pray
The curse I laid on others fall on me.
See that ye give effect to all my hest,

For my sake and the god's and for our land,
A desert blasted by the wrath of heaven.
For, let alone the god's express command,
It were a scandal ye should leave unpurged
The murder of a great man and your king,
Nor track it home. And now that I am lord, 260
Successor to his throne, his bed, his wife,
(And had he not been frustrate in the hope
Of issue, common children of one womb
Had forced a closer bond twixt him and me,
But Fate swooped down upon him), therefore I
His blood-avenger will maintain his cause
As though he were my sire, and leave no stone
Unturned to track the assassin or avenge
The son of Labdacus, of Polydore,
Of Cadmus, and Agenor first of the race. 270
And for the disobedient thus I pray:
May the gods send them neither timely fruits
Of earth, nor teeming increase of the womb,
But may they waste and pine, as now they waste,
Aye and worse stricken; but to all of you,
My loyal subjects who approve my acts,
May Justice, our ally, and all the gods
Be gracious and attend you evermore.

CHORUS
The oath thou profferest, sire, I take and swear.
I slew him not myself, nor can I name 280
The slayer. For the quest, 'twere well, methinks
That Phoebus, who proposed the riddle, himself
Should give the answer—who the murderer was.

OEDIPUS
Well argued; but no living man can hope
To force the gods to speak against their will.

CHORUS
May I then say what seems next best to me?

OEDIPUS
Aye, if there be a third best, tell it too.

CHORUS

My liege, if any man sees eye to eye
With our lord Phoebus, 'tis our prophet, lord
Teiresias; he of all men best might guide   2 ℞
A searcher of this matter to the light.

OEDIPUS
Here too my zeal has nothing lagged, for twice
At Creon's instance have I sent to fetch him,
And long I marvel why he is not here.

CHORUS
I mind me too of rumors long ago—
Mere gossip.

OEDIPUS
             Tell them, I would fain know all.

CHORUS
'Twas said he fell by travelers.

OEDIPUS
                    So I heard,
But none has seen the man who saw him fall.

CHORUS
Well, if he knows what fear is, he will quail   300
And flee before the terror of thy curse.

OEDIPUS
Words scare not him who blenches not at deeds.

CHORUS
But here is one to arraign him. Lo, at length
They bring the god-inspired seer in whom
Above all other men is truth inborn.
[Enter TEIRESIAS, led by a boy.]

OEDIPUS
Teiresias, seer who comprehendest all,
Lore of the wise and hidden mysteries,
High things of heaven and low things of the earth, ℞
Thou knowest, though thy blinded eyes see naught,
What plague infects our city; and we turn

To thee, O seer, our one defense and shield.
The purport of the answer that the God
Returned to us who sought his oracle,
The messengers have doubtless told thee—how
One course alone could rid us of the pest,
To find the murderers of Laius,
And slay them or expel them from the land.
Therefore begrudging neither augury
Nor other divination that is thine,
O save thyself, thy country, and thy king,
Save all from this defilement of blood shed.
On thee we rest. This is man's highest end,
To others' service all his powers to lend.

TEIRESIAS
Alas, alas, what misery to be wise
When wisdom profits nothing! This old lore
I had forgotten; else I were not here.

OEDIPUS
What ails thee? Why this melancholy mood?

TEIRESIAS
Let me go home; prevent me not; 'twere best
That thou shouldst bear thy burden and I mine.

OEDIPUS
For shame! no true-born Theban patriot
Would thus withhold the word of prophecy.

TEIRESIAS
Thy words, O king, are wide of the mark, and I
For fear lest I too trip like thee...

OEDIPUS
                    Oh speak,
Withhold not, I adjure thee, if thou know'st,
Thy knowledge. We are all thy suppliants.

TEIRESIAS
Aye, for ye all are witless, but my voice
Will ne'er reveal my miseries—or thine. 2

OEDIPUS
What then, thou knowest, and yet willst not speak!
Wouldst thou betray us and destroy the State?   3 30

TEIRESIAS
I will not vex myself nor thee. Why ask
Thus idly what from me thou shalt not learn?

OEDIPUS
Monster! thy silence would incense a flint.
Will nothing loose thy tongue? Can nothing melt thee,
Or shake thy dogged taciturnity?

TEIRESIAS
Thou blam'st my mood and seest not thine own
Wherewith thou art mated; no, thou taxest me.

OEDIPUS
And who could stay his choler when he heard
How insolently thou dost flout the State?

TEIRESIAS
Well, it will come what will, though I be mute.   3 40

OEDIPUS
Since come it must, thy duty is to tell me.

TEIRESIAS
I have no more to say; storm as thou willst,
And give the rein to all thy pent-up rage.

OEDIPUS
Yea, I am wroth, and will not stint my words,
But speak my whole mind. Thou methinks thou art he,
Who planned the crime, aye, and performed it too,
All save the assassination; and if thou
Hadst not been blind, I had been sworn to boot
That thou alone didst do the bloody deed.

TEIRESIAS
Is it so? Then I charge thee to abide
By thine own proclamation; from this day
Speak not to these or me. Thou art the man,

Thou the accursed polluter of this land.

OEDIPUS
Vile slanderer, thou blurtest forth these taunts,
And think'st forsooth as seer to go scot free.

TEIRESIAS
Yea, I am free, strong in the strength of truth.

OEDIPUS
Who was thy teacher? not methinks thy art.

TEIRESIAS
Thou, goading me against my will to speak.

OEDIPUS
What speech? repeat it and resolve my doubt.

TEIRESIAS
Didst miss my sense wouldst thou goad me on?

OEDIPUS
I but half caught thy meaning; say it again.   *3 60*

TEIRESIAS
I say thou art the murderer of the man
Whose murderer thou pursuest.

OEDIPUS
                    Thou shalt rue it
Twice to repeat so gross a calumny.

TEIRESIAS
Must I say more to aggravate thy rage?

OEDIPUS
Say all thou wilt; it will be but waste of breath.

TEIRESIAS
I say thou livest with thy nearest kin
In infamy, unwitting in thy shame.

OEDIPUS

Think'st thou for aye unscathed to wag thy tongue? 320

TEIRESIAS
Yea, if the might of truth can aught prevail.
OEDIPUS
With other men, but not with thee, for thou
In ear, wit, eye, in everything art blind.

TEIRESIAS
Poor fool to utter gibes at me which all
Here present will cast back on thee ere long.

OEDIPUS
Offspring of endless Night, thou hast no power
O'er me or any man who sees the sun.

TEIRESIAS
No, for thy weird is not to fall by me.
I leave to Apollo what concerns the god.

OEDIPUS
Is this a plot of Creon, or thine own? 280

TEIRESIAS
Not Creon, thou thyself art thine own bane.

OEDIPUS
O wealth and empiry and skill by skill
Outwitted in the battlefield of life,
What spite and envy follow in your train!
See, for this crown the State conferred on me.
A gift, a thing I sought not, for this crown
The trusty Creon, my familiar friend,
Hath lain in wait to oust me and suborned
This mountebank, this juggling charlatan,
This tricksy beggar-priest, for gain alone 390
Keen-eyed, but in his proper art stone-blind.
Say, sirrah, hast thou ever proved thyself
A prophet? When the riddling Sphinx was here
Why hadst thou no deliverance for this folk?
And yet the riddle was not to be solved
By guess-work but required the prophet's art;
Wherein thou wast found lacking; neither birds

Nor sign from heaven helped thee, but I came,
The simple Oedipus; I stopped her mouth
By mother wit, untaught of auguries.
This is the man whom thou wouldst undermine,
In hope to reign with Creon in my stead.
Methinks that thou and thine abettor soon
Will rue your plot to drive the scapegoat out.
Thank thy grey hairs that thou hast still to learn
What chastisement such arrogance deserves.

CHORUS
To us it seems that both the seer and thou,
O Oedipus, have spoken angry words.
This is no time to wrangle but consult
How best we may fulfill the oracle.

TEIRESIAS
King as thou art, free speech at least is mine
To make reply; in this I am thy peer.
I own no lord but Loxias; him I serve
And ne'er can stand enrolled as Creon's man.
Thus then I answer: since thou hast not spared
To twit me with my blindness—thou hast eyes,
Yet see'st not in what misery thou art fallen,
Nor where thou dwellest nor with whom for mate.
Dost know thy lineage? Nay, thou know'st it not,
And all unwitting art a double foe
To thine own kin, the living and the dead;
Aye and the dogging curse of mother and sire
One day shall drive thee, like a two-edged sword,
Beyond our borders, and the eyes that now
See clear shall henceforward endless night.
Ah whither shall thy bitter cry not reach,
What crag in all Cithaeron but shall then
Reverberate thy wail, when thou hast found
With what a hymeneal thou wast borne
Home, but to no fair haven, on the gale!
Aye, and a flood of ills thou guessest not
Shall set thyself and children in one line.
Flout then both Creon and my words, for none
Of mortals shall be striken worse than thou.

OEDIPUS

Must I endure this fellow's insolence?
A murrain on thee! Get thee hence! Begone
Avaunt! and never cross my threshold more.

TEIRESIAS
I ne'er had come hadst thou not bidden me.

OEDIPUS
I know not thou wouldst utter folly, else
Long hadst thou waited to be summoned here.

TEIRESIAS
Such am I—as it seems to thee a fool,
But to the parents who begat thee, wise.

OEDIPUS
What sayest thou—"parents"? Who begat me, speak?

TEIRESIAS
This day shall be thy birth-day, and thy grave.

OEDIPUS
Thou lov'st to speak in riddles and dark words.

TEIRESIAS
In reading riddles who so skilled as thou?

OEDIPUS
Twit me with that wherein my greatness lies.

TEIRESIAS
And yet this very greatness proved thy bane.

OEDIPUS
No matter if I saved the commonwealth.

TEIRESIAS
'Tis time I left thee. Come, boy, take me home.

OEDIPUS
Aye, take him quickly, for his presence irks
And lets me; gone, thou canst not plague me more.

TEIRESIAS

I go, but first will tell thee why I came.
Thy frown I dread not, for thou canst not harm me.
Hear then: this man whom thou hast sought to arrest
With threats and warrants this long while, the wretch
Who murdered Laius—that man is here.
He passes for an alien in the land
But soon shall prove a Theban, native born.
And yet his fortune brings him little joy;
For blind of seeing, clad in beggar's weeds,
For purple robes, and leaning on his staff,
To a strange land he soon shall grope his way.
And of the children, inmates of his home,   460
He shall be proved the brother and the sire,
Of her who bare him son and husband both,
Co-partner, and assassin of his sire.
Go in and ponder this, and if thou find
That I have missed the mark, henceforth declare
I have no wit nor skill in prophecy.
[Exeunt TEIRESIAS and OEDIPUS]

CHORUS
(Str. 1)
Who is he by voice immortal named from Pythia's rocky
cell,
Doer of foul deeds of bloodshed, horrors that no tongue
can tell?   470
          A foot for flight he needs
          Fleeter than storm-swift steeds,
          For on his heels doth follow,
Armed with the lightnings of his Sire, Apollo.
          Like sleuth-hounds too
          The Fates pursue.

(Ant. 1)
Yea, but now flashed forth the summons from Parnassus'
snowy peak,
"Near and far the undiscovered doer of this murder
seek!"   480
          Now like a sullen bull he roves
          Through forest brakes and upland groves,
          And vainly seeks to fly
          The doom that ever nigh

Flits o'er his head,
Still by the avenging Phoebus sped,
The voice divine,
From Earth's mid shrine.

(Str. 2)

Sore perplexed am I by the words of the master seer.
Are they true, are they false? I know not and bridle my
tongue for
fear,
Fluttered with vague surmise; nor present nor future is
clear.
Quarrel of ancient date or in days still near know I none
Twixt the Labdacidan house and our ruler, Polybus' son.
Proof is there none: how then can I challenge our King's
good name,
How in a blood-feud join for an untracked deed of
shame?

(Ant. 2)

All wise are Zeus and Apollo, and nothing is hid from
their ken;
They are gods; and in wits a man may surpass his fellow
men;
But that a mortal seer knows more than I know—where
Hath this been proven? Or how without sign assured,
can I blame
Him who saved our State when the winged songstress
came,
Tested and tried in the light of us all, like gold assayed?
How can I now assent when a crime is on Oedipus laid?

CREON

Friends, countrymen, I learn King Oedipus
Hath laid against me a most grievous charge,
And come to you protesting. If he deems
That I have harmed or injured him in aught
By word or deed in this our present trouble,
I care not to prolong the span of life,
Thus ill-reputed; for the calumny
Hits not a single blot, but blasts my name,
If by the general voice I am denounced
False to the State and false by you my friends.

CHORUS
This taunt, it well may be, was blurted out
In petulance, not spoken advisedly.

CREON
Did any dare pretend that it was I
Prompted the seer to utter a forged charge?

CHORUS
Such things were said; with what intent I know not.

CREON
Were not his wits and vision all astray
When upon me he fixed this monstrous charge?

CHORUS
I know not; to my sovereign's acts I am blind.
But lo, he comes to answer for himself.
[Enter OEDIPUS.]

OEDIPUS
Sirrah, what mak'st thou here? Dost thou presume
To approach my doors, thou brazen-faced rogue,
My murderer and the filcher of my crown?
Come, answer this, didst thou detect in me
Some touch of cowardice or witlessness,
That made thee undertake this enterprise?
I seemed forsooth too simple to perceive
The serpent stealing on me in the dark,
Or else too weak to scotch it when I saw.
This thou art witless seeking to possess
Without a following or friends the crown,
A prize that followers and wealth must win.

CREON
Attend me. Thou hast spoken, 'tis my turn
To make reply. Then having heard me, judge.

OEDIPUS
Thou art glib of tongue, but I am slow to learn
Of thee; I know too well thy venomous hate.

CREON

First I would argue out this very point.

OEDIPUS
O argue not that thou art not a rogue.

CREON
If thou dost count a virtue stubbornness,
Unschooled by reason, thou art much astray.

OEDIPUS
If thou dost hold a kinsman may be wronged,
And no pains follow, thou art much to seek.   40

CREON
Therein thou judgest rightly, but this wrong
That thou allegest—tell me what it is.

OEDIPUS
Didst thou or didst thou not advise that I
Should call the priest?

CREON
                          Yes, and I stand to it.

OEDIPUS
Tell me how long is it since Laius...

CREON
Since Laius...? I follow not thy drift.

OEDIPUS
By violent hands was spirited away.

CREON
In the dim past, a many years agone.

OEDIPUS
Did the same prophet then pursue his craft? 350

CREON
Yes, skilled as now and in no less repute.

OEDIPUS

Did he at that time ever glance at me?

CREON
Not to my knowledge, not when I was by.

OEDIPUS
But was no search and inquisition made?

CREON
Surely full quest was made, but nothing learnt.

OEDIPUS
Why failed the seer to tell his story then?

CREON
I know not, and not knowing hold my tongue.

OEDIPUS
This much thou knowest and canst surely tell.

CREON
What's mean'st thou? All I know I will declare.

OEDIPUS
But for thy prompting never had the seer
Ascribed to me the death of Laius.

CREON
If so he thou knowest best; but I
Would put thee to the question in my turn.

OEDIPUS
Question and prove me murderer if thou canst.

CREON
Then let me ask thee, didst thou wed my sister?

OEDIPUS
A fact so plain I cannot well deny.

CREON
And as thy consort queen she shares the throne?

OEDIPUS
I grant her freely all her heart desires.

CREON
And with you twain I share the triple rule?

OEDIPUS
Yea, and it is that proves thee a false friend.

CREON
Not so, if thou wouldst reason with thyself,   570
As I with myself. First, I bid thee think,
Would any mortal choose a troubled reign
Of terrors rather than secure repose,
If the same power were given him? As for me,
I have no natural craving for the name
Of king, preferring to do kingly deeds,
And so thinks every sober-minded man.
Now all my needs are satisfied through thee,
And I have naught to fear; but were I king,
My acts would oft run counter to my will.   580
How could a title then have charms for me
Above the sweets of boundless influence?
I am not so infatuate as to grasp
The shadow when I hold the substance fast.
Now all men cry me Godspeed! wish me well,
And every suitor seeks to gain my ear,
If he would hope to win a grace from thee.
Why should I leave the better, choose the worse?
That were sheer madness, and I am not mad.
No such ambition ever tempted me,   590
Nor would I have a share in such intrigue.
And if thou doubt me, first to Delphi go,
There ascertain if my report was true
Of the god's answer; next investigate
If with the seer I plotted or conspired,
And if it prove so, sentence me to death,
Not by thy voice alone, but mine and thine.
But O condemn me not, without appeal,
On bare suspicion. 'Tis not right to adjudge
Bad men at random good, or good men bad.   600
I would as lief a man should cast away
The thing he counts most precious, his own life,

As spurn a true friend. Thou wilt learn in time
The truth, for time alone reveals the just;
A villain is detected in a day.

CHORUS
To one who walketh warily his words
Commend themselves; swift counsels are not sure.

OEDIPUS
When with swift strides the stealthy plotter stalks
I must be quick too with my counterplot.
To wait his onset passively, for him
Is sure success, for me assured defeat.

CREON
What then's thy will? To banish me the land?

OEDIPUS
I would not have thee banished, no, but dead,
That men may mark the wages envy reaps.

CREON
I see thou wilt not yield, nor credit me.

OEDIPUS
[None but a fool would credit such as thou.] 3

CREON
Thou art not wise.

OEDIPUS
                Wise for myself at least.

CREON
Why not for me too?

OEDIPUS
                Why for such a knave?

CREON
Suppose thou lackest sense.

OEDIPUS

Yet kings must rule.

CREON
Not if they rule ill.

OEDIPUS
                    Oh my Thebans, hear him!

CREON
Thy Thebans? am not I a Theban too?

CHORUS
Cease, princes; lo there comes, and none too soon,
Jocasta from the palace. Who so fit
As peacemaker to reconcile your feud?
[Enter JOCASTA.]

JOCASTA
Misguided princes, why have ye upraised
This wordy wrangle? Are ye not ashamed,
While the whole land lies striken, thus to voice
Your private injuries? Go in, my lord;
Go home, my brother, and forebear to make
A public scandal of a petty grief.

CREON
My royal sister, Oedipus, thy lord,
Hath bid me choose (O dread alternative!)
An outlaw's exile or a felon's death.

OEDIPUS
Yes, lady; I have caught him practicing
Against my royal person his vile arts.

CREON
May I ne'er speed but die accursed, if I
In any way am guilty of this charge.

JOCASTA
Believe him, I adjure thee, Oedipus,
First for his solemn oath's sake, then for mine,
And for thine elders' sake who wait on thee.

CHORUS
(Str. 1)
Hearken, King, reflect, we pray thee, but not stubborn
but relent.

OEDIPUS
Say to what should I consent?

CHORUS
Respect a man whose probity and troth
Are known to all and now confirmed by oath.

OEDIPUS
Dost know what grace thou cravest?

CHORUS
                    Yea, I know.

OEDIPUS
Declare it then and make thy meaning plain.

CHORUS
Brand not a friend whom babbling tongues assail;
Let not suspicion 'gainst his oath prevail.

OEDIPUS
Bethink you that in seeking this ye seek
In very sooth my death or banishment?

CHORUS
No, by the leader of the host divine!
(Str. 2)
Witness, thou Sun, such thought was never mine,
Unblest, unfriended may I perish,
If ever I such wish did cherish!
But O my heart is desolate
Musing on our striken State,
Doubly fall'n should discord grow
Twixt you twain, to crown our woe.

OEDIPUS
Well, let him go, no matter what it cost me,
Or certain death or shameful banishment,

For your sake I relent, not his; and him,
Where'er he be, my heart shall still abhor.

CREON
Thou art as sullen in thy yielding mood   670
As in thine anger thou wast truculent.
Such tempers justly plague themselves the most.

OEDIPUS
Leave me in peace and get thee gone.

CREON
                    I go,
By thee misjudged, but justified by these.
[Exeunt CREON]

CHORUS
(Ant. 1)
Lady, lead indoors thy consort; wherefore longer here
delay?

JOCASTA
Tell me first how rose the fray.

CHORUS
Rumors bred unjust suspicious and injustice rankles sore.

JOCASTA
Were both at fault?   680

CHORUS
                Both.

JOCASTA
                    What was the tale?

CHORUS
Ask me no more. The land is sore distressed;
'Twere better sleeping ills to leave at rest.

OEDIPUS
Strange counsel, friend! I know thou mean'st me well,
And yet would'st mitigate and blunt my zeal.

CHORUS
(Ant. 2)
King, I say it once again,
Witless were I proved, insane,
If I lightly put away
Thee my country's prop and stay,   6 90
Pilot who, in danger sought,
To a quiet haven brought
Our distracted State; and now
Who can guide us right but thou?

JOCASTA
Let me too, I adjure thee, know, O king,
What cause has stirred this unrelenting wrath.

OEDIPUS
I will, for thou art more to me than these.
Lady, the cause is Creon and his plots.

JOCASTA
But what provoked the quarrel? make this clear.

OEDIPUS
He points me out as Laius' murderer.   700

JOCASTA
Of his own knowledge or upon report?

OEDIPUS
He is too cunning to commit himself,
And makes a mouthpiece of a knavish seer.

JOCASTA
Then thou mayest ease thy conscience on that score.
Listen and I'll convince thee that no man
Hath scot or lot in the prophetic art.
Here is the proof in brief. An oracle
Once came to Laius (I will not say
'Twas from the Delphic god himself, but from
His ministers) declaring he was doomed   710
To perish by the hand of his own son,
A child that should be born to him by me.

Now Laius—so at least report affirmed—
Was murdered on a day by highwaymen,
No natives, at a spot where three roads meet.
As for the child, it was but three days old,
When Laius, its ankles pierced and pinned
Together, gave it to be cast away
By others on the trackless mountain side.
So then Apollo brought it not to pass   820
The child should be his father's murderer,
Or the dread terror find accomplishment,
And Laius be slain by his own son.
Such was the prophet's horoscope. O king,
Regard it not. Whate'er the god deems fit
To search, himself unaided will reveal.

OEDIPUS
What memories, what wild tumult of the soul
Came o'er me, lady, as I heard thee speak!

JOCASTA
What mean'st thou? What has shocked and startled thee?

OEDIPUS
Methought I heard thee say that Laius   830
Was murdered at the meeting of three roads.

JOCASTA
So ran the story that is current still.

OEDIPUS
Where did this happen? Dost thou know the place?

JOCASTA
Phocis the land is called; the spot is where
Branch roads from Delphi and from Daulis meet.

OEDIPUS
And how long is it since these things befell?

JOCASTA
'Twas but a brief while were thou wast proclaimed
Our country's ruler that the news was brought.

OEDIPUS
O Zeus, what hast thou willed to do with me!

JOCASTA
What is it, Oedipus, that moves thee so?   740

OEDIPUS
Ask me not yet; tell me the build and height
Of Laius? Was he still in manhood's prime?

JOCASTA
Tall was he, and his hair was lightly strewn
With silver; and not unlike thee in form.

OEDIPUS
O woe is me! Mehtinks unwittingly
I laid but now a dread curse on myself.

JOCASTA
What say'st thou? When I look upon thee, my king,
I tremble.

OEDIPUS
        'Tis a dread presentiment
That in the end the seer will prove not blind.   750
One further question to resolve my doubt.

JOCASTA
I quail; but ask, and I will answer all.

OEDIPUS
Had he but few attendants or a train
Of armed retainers with him, like a prince?

JOCASTA
They were but five in all, and one of them
A herald; Laius in a mule-car rode.

OEDIPUS
Alas! 'tis clear as noonday now. But say,
Lady, who carried this report to Thebes?

JOCASTA

A serf, the sole survivor who returned.

OEDIPUS
Haply he is at hand or in the house?   260

JOCASTA
No, for as soon as he returned and found
Thee reigning in the stead of Laius slain,
He clasped my hand and supplicated me
To send him to the alps and pastures, where
He might be farthest from the sight of Thebes.
And so I sent him. 'Twas an honest slave
And well deserved some better recompense.

OEDIPUS
Fetch him at once. I fain would see the man.

JOCASTA
He shall be brought; but wherefore summon him?

OEDIPUS
Lady, I fear my tongue has overrun   270
Discretion; therefore I would question him.

JOCASTA
Well, he shall come, but may not I too claim
To share the burden of thy heart, my king?

OEDIPUS
And thou shalt not be frustrate of thy wish.
Now my imaginings have gone so far.
Who has a higher claim that thou to hear
My tale of dire adventures? Listen then.
My sire was Polybus of Corinth, and
My mother Merope, a Dorian;
And I was held the foremost citizen,   780
Till a strange thing befell me, strange indeed,
Yet scarce deserving all the heat it stirred.
A roisterer at some banquet, flown with wine,
Shouted "Thou art not true son of thy sire."
It irked me, but I stomached for the nonce
The insult; on the morrow I sought out
My mother and my sire and questioned them.

They were indignant at the random slur
Cast on my parentage and did their best
To comfort me, but still the venomed barb 790
Rankled, for still the scandal spread and grew.
So privily without their leave I went
To Delphi, and Apollo sent me back
Baulked of the knowledge that I came to seek.
But other grievous things he prophesied,
Woes, lamentations, mourning, portents dire;
To wit I should defile my mother's bed
And raise up seed too loathsome to behold,
And slay the father from whose loins I sprang.
Then, lady,—thou shalt hear the very truth— 800
As I drew near the triple-branching roads,
A herald met me and a man who sat
In a car drawn by colts—as in thy tale—
The man in front and the old man himself
Threatened to thrust me rudely from the path,
Then jostled by the charioteer in wrath
I struck him, and the old man, seeing this,
Watched till I passed and from his car brought down
Full on my head the double-pointed goad.
    Yet was I quits with him and more; one stroke 810
Of my good staff sufficed to fling him clean
Out of the chariot seat and laid him prone.
And so I slew them every one. But if
Betwixt this stranger there was aught in common
With Laius, who more miserable than I,
What mortal could you find more god-abhorred?
Wretch whom no sojourner, no citizen
May harbor or address, whom all are bound
To harry from their homes. And this same curse
Was laid on me, and laid by none but me. 820
Yea with these hands all gory I pollute
The bed of him I slew. Say, am I vile?
Am I not utterly unclean, a wretch
Doomed to be banished, and in banishment
Forgo the sight of all my dearest ones,
And never tread again my native earth;
Or else to wed my mother and slay my sire,
Polybus, who begat me and upreared?
If one should say, this is the handiwork
Of some inhuman power, who could blame 830

His judgment? But, ye pure and awful gods,
Forbid, forbid that I should see that day!
May I be blotted out from living men
Ere such a plague spot set on me its brand!

CHORUS
We too, O king, are troubled; but till thou
Hast questioned the survivor, still hope on.

OEDIPUS
My hope is faint, but still enough survives
To bid me bide the coming of this herd.

JOCASTA
Suppose him here, what wouldst thou learn of him?

OEDIPUS
I'll tell thee, lady; if his tale agrees
With thine, I shall have 'scaped calamity.

JOCASTA
And what of special import did I say?

OEDIPUS
In thy report of what the herdsman said
Laius was slain by robbers; now if he
Still speaks of robbers, not a robber, I
Slew him not; "one" with "many" cannot square.
But if he says one lonely wayfarer,
The last link wanting to my guilt is forged.

JOCASTA
Well, rest assured, his tale ran thus at first,
Nor can he now retract what then he said;
Not I alone but all our townsfolk heard it.
E'en should he vary somewhat in his story,
He cannot make the death of Laius
In any wise jump with the oracle.
For Loxias said expressly he was doomed
To die by my child's hand, but he, poor babe,
He shed no blood, but perished first himself.
So much for divination. Henceforth I
Will look for signs neither to right nor left.

OEDIPUS
Thou reasonest well. Still I would have thee send   860
And fetch the bondsman hither. See to it.

JOCASTA
That will I straightway. Come, let us within.
I would do nothing that my lord mislikes.
[Exeunt OEDIPUS and JOCASTA]

CHORUS
(Str. 1)
My lot be still to lead
    The life of innocence and fly
Irreverence in word or deed,
    To follow still those laws ordained on high
Whose birthplace is the bright ethereal sky
    No mortal birth they own,
    Olympus their progenitor alone: 870
Ne'er shall they slumber in oblivion cold,
The god in them is strong and grows not old.

(Ant. 1)
    Of insolence is bred
The tyrant; insolence full blown,
    With empty riches surfeited,
Scales the precipitous height and grasps the throne.
    Then topples o'er and lies in ruin prone;
    No foothold on that dizzy steep.
But O may Heaven the true patriot keep
Who burns with emulous zeal to serve the State.   880
God is my help and hope, on him I wait.

(Str. 2)
But the proud sinner, or in word or deed,
    That will not Justice heed,
    Nor reverence the shrine
    Of images divine,
Perdition seize his vain imaginings,
    If, urged by greed profane,
    He grasps at ill-got gain,
And lays an impious hand on holiest things.
    Who when such deeds are done   890

Can hope heaven's bolts to shun?
If sin like this to honor can aspire,
Why dance I still and lead the sacred choir?

(Ant. 2)
No more I'll seek earth's central oracle,
    Or Abae's hallowed cell,
    Nor to Olympia bring
    My votive offering.
If before all God's truth be not bade plain.
    O Zeus, reveal thy might,
    King, if thou'rt named aright
Omnipotent, all-seeing, as of old;
    For Laius is forgot;
    His weird, men heed it not;
Apollo is forsook and faith grows cold.
[Enter JOCASTA.]

JOCASTA
My lords, ye look amazed to see your queen
With wreaths and gifts of incense in her hands.
I had a mind to visit the high shrines,
For Oedipus is overwrought, alarmed
With terrors manifold. He will not use
His past experience, like a man of sense,
To judge the present need, but lends an ear
To any croaker if he augurs ill.
Since then my counsels naught avail, I turn
To thee, our present help in time of trouble,
Apollo, Lord Lycean, and to thee
My prayers and supplications here I bring.
Lighten us, lord, and cleanse us from this curse!
For now we all are cowed like mariners
Who see their helmsman dumbstruck in the storm.
[Enter Corinthian MESSENGER.]

MESSENGER
My masters, tell me where the palace is
Of Oedipus; or better, where's the king.

CHORUS
Here is the palace and he bides within;
This is his queen the mother of his children.

MESSENGER
All happiness attend her and the house,
Blessed is her husband and her marriage-bed.

JOCASTA
My greetings to thee, stranger; thy fair words
Deserve a like response. But tell me why
Thou comest—what thy need or what thy news.

MESSENGER
Good for thy consort and the royal house.

JOCASTA
What may it be? Whose messenger art thou? 930

MESSENGER
The Isthmian commons have resolved to make
Thy husband king—so 'twas reported there.

JOCASTA
What! is not aged Polybus still king?

MESSENGER
No, verily; he's dead and in his grave.

JOCASTA
What! is he dead, the sire of Oedipus?

MESSENGER
If I speak falsely, may I die myself.

JOCASTA
Quick, maiden, bear these tidings to my lord.
Ye god-sent oracles, where stand ye now!
This is the man whom Oedipus long shunned,
In dread to prove his murderer; and now 940
He dies in nature's course, not by his hand.
[Enter OEDIPUS.]

OEDIPUS
My wife, my queen, Jocasta, why hast thou
Summoned me from my palace?

JOCASTA

Hear this man,
And as thou hearest judge what has become
Of all those awe-inspiring oracles.

OEDIPUS

Who is this man, and what his news for me?

JOCASTA

He comes from Corinth and his message this:
Thy father Polybus hath passed away.   950

OEDIPUS

What? let me have it, stranger, from thy mouth.

MESSENGER

If I must first make plain beyond a doubt
My message, know that Polybus is dead.

OEDIPUS

By treachery, or by sickness visited?

MESSENGER

One touch will send an old man to his rest.

OEDIPUS

So of some malady he died, poor man.

MESSENGER

Yes, having measured the full span of years.

OEDIPUS

Out on it, lady! why should one regard
The Pythian hearth or birds that scream i' the air?
Did they not point at me as doomed to slay   960
My father? but he's dead and in his grave
And here am I who ne'er unsheathed a sword;
Unless the longing for his absent son
Killed him and so I slew him in a sense.
But, as they stand, the oracles are dead—
Dust, ashes, nothing, dead as Polybus.

JOCASTA
Say, did not I foretell this long ago?

OEDIPUS
Thou didst: but I was misled by my fear.

JOCASTA
Then let I no more weigh upon thy soul.

OEDIPUS
Must I not fear my mother's marriage bed.   970

JOCASTA
Why should a mortal man, the sport of chance,
With no assured foreknowledge, be afraid?
Best live a careless life from hand to mouth.
This wedlock with thy mother fear not thou.
How oft it chances that in dreams a man
Has wed his mother! He who least regards
Such brainsick phantasies lives most at ease.

OEDIPUS
I should have shared in full thy confidence,
Were not my mother living; since she lives
Though half convinced I still must live in dread.   980

JOCASTA
And yet thy sire's death lights out darkness much.

OEDIPUS
Much, but my fear is touching her who lives.

MESSENGER
Who may this woman be whom thus you fear?

OEDIPUS
Merope, stranger, wife of Polybus.

MESSENGER
And what of her can cause you any fear?

OEDIPUS
A heaven-sent oracle of dread import.

MESSENGER
A mystery, or may a stranger hear it?

OEDIPUS
Aye, 'tis no secret. Loxias once foretold
That I should mate with mine own mother, and shed
With my own hands the blood of my own sire.
Hence Corinth was for many a year to me   990
A home distant; and I trove abroad,
But missed the sweetest sight, my parents' face.

MESSENGER
Was this the fear that exiled thee from home?

OEDIPUS
Yea, and the dread of slaying my own sire.

MESSENGER
Why, since I came to give thee pleasure, King,
Have I not rid thee of this second fear?

OEDIPUS
Well, thou shalt have due guerdon for thy pains.

MESSENGER
Well, I confess what chiefly made me come
Was hope to profit by thy coming home.

OEDIPUS
Nay, I will ne'er go near my parents more.   1000

MESSENGER
My son, 'tis plain, thou know'st not what thou doest.

OEDIPUS
How so, old man? For heaven's sake tell me all.

MESSENGER
If this is why thou dreadest to return.

OEDIPUS
Yea, lest the god's word be fulfilled in me.

MESSENGER
Lest through thy parents thou shouldst be accursed?

OEDIPUS
This and none other is my constant dread.

MESSENGER
Dost thou not know thy fears are baseless all?

OEDIPUS
How baseless, if I am their very son?

MESSENGER
Since Polybus was naught to thee in blood.

OEDIPUS
What say'st thou? was not Polybus my sire?   1110

MESSENGER
As much thy sire as I am, and no more.

OEDIPUS
My sire no more to me than one who is naught?

MESSENGER
Since I begat thee not, no more did he.

OEDIPUS
What reason had he then to call me son?

MESSENGER
Know that he took thee from my hands, a gift.

OEDIPUS
Yet, if no child of his, he loved me well.

MESSENGER
A childless man till then, he warmed to thee.

OEDIPUS
A foundling or a purchased slave, this child?

MESSENGER
I found thee in Cithaeron's wooded glens.

OEDIPUS
What led thee to explore those upland glades?

MESSENGER
My business was to tend the mountain flocks.

OEDIPUS
A vagrant shepherd journeying for hire?

MESSENGER
True, but thy savior in that hour, my son.

OEDIPUS
My savior? from what harm? what ailed me then?

MESSENGER
Those ankle joints are evidence enow.

OEDIPUS
Ah, why remind me of that ancient sore?

MESSENGER
I loosed the pin that riveted thy feet.

OEDIPUS
Yes, from my cradle that dread brand I bore.

MESSENGER
Whence thou deriv'st the name that still is thine.

OEDIPUS
Who did it? I adjure thee, tell me who
Say, was it father, mother?

MESSENGER
                    I know not.
The man from whom I had thee may know more.

OEDIPUS
What, did another find me, not thyself?

MESSENGER
Not I; another shepherd gave thee me.

OEDIPUS
Who was he? Would'st thou know again the man?

MESSENGER
He passed indeed for one of Laius' house.

OEDIPUS
The king who ruled the country long ago?

MESSENGER
The same: he was a herdsman of the king.

OEDIPUS
And is he living still for me to see him?   1140

MESSENGER
His fellow-countrymen should best know that.

OEDIPUS
Doth any bystander among you know
The herd he speaks of, or by seeing him
Afield or in the city? answer straight!
The hour hath come to clear this business up.

CHORUS
Methinks he means none other than the hind
Whom thou anon wert fain to see; but that
Our queen Jocasta best of all could tell.

OEDIPUS
Madam, dost know the man we sent to fetch?
Is the same of whom the stranger speaks?   1150

JOCASTA
Who is the man? What matter? Let it be.
'Twere waste of thought to weigh such idle words.

OEDIPUS
No, with such guiding clues I cannot fail

To bring to light the secret of my birth.

JOCASTA
Oh, as thou carest for thy life, give o'er
This quest. Enough the anguish I endure.

OEDIPUS
Be of good cheer; though I be proved the son
Of a bondwoman, aye, through three descents
Triply a slave, thy honor is unsmirched.

JOCASTA
Yet humor me, I pray thee; do not this.   1160

OEDIPUS
I cannot; I must probe this matter home.

JOCASTA
'Tis for thy sake I advise thee for the best.

OEDIPUS
I grow impatient of this best advice.

JOCASTA
Ah mayst thou ne'er discover who thou art!

OEDIPUS
Go, fetch me here the herd, and leave yon woman
To glory in her pride of ancestry.

JOCASTA
O woe is thee, poor wretch! With that last word
I leave thee, henceforth silent evermore.
[Exit JOCASTA]

CHORUS
Why, Oedipus, why stung with passionate grief
Hath the queen thus departed? Much I fear   1170
From this dead calm will burst a storm of woes.

OEDIPUS
Let the storm burst, my fixed resolve still holds,
To learn my lineage, be it ne'er so low.

It may be she with all a woman's pride
Thinks scorn of my base parentage. But I
Who rank myself as Fortune's favorite child,
The giver of good gifts, shall not be shamed.
She is my mother and the changing moons
My brethren, and with them I wax and wane.
Thus sprung why should I fear to trace my birth?   11 80
Nothing can make me other than I am.

CHORUS
(Str.)
If my soul prophetic err not, if my wisdom aught avail,
     Thee, Cithaeron, I shall hail,
As the nurse and foster-mother of our Oedipus shall
greet
Ere tomorrow's full moon rises, and exalt thee as is meet.
Dance and song shall hymn thy praises, lover of our
royal race.
     Phoebus, may my words find grace!

(Ant.)
Child, who bare thee, nymph or goddess? sure thy sure   1190
was more than
man,
     Haply the hill-roamer Pan.
Of did Loxias beget thee, for he haunts the upland wold;
Or Cyllene's lord, or Bacchus, dweller on the hilltops
cold?
Did some Heliconian Oread give him thee, a new-born
joy?
     Nymphs with whom he love to toy?

OEDIPUS   1200
Elders, if I, who never yet before
Have met the man, may make a guess, methinks
I see the herdsman who we long have sought;
His time-worn aspect matches with the years
Of yonder aged messenger; besides
I seem to recognize the men who bring him
As servants of my own. But you, perchance,
Having in past days known or seen the herd,
May better by sure knowledge my surmise.

CHORUS
I recognize him; one of Laius' house;
A simple hind, but true as any man.   *1200*
[Enter HERDSMAN.]

OEDIPUS
Corinthian, stranger, I address thee first,
Is this the man thou meanest!

MESSENGER
                        This is he.

OEDIPUS
And now old man, look up and answer all
I ask thee. Wast thou once of Laius' house?

HERDSMAN
I was, a thrall, not purchased but home-bred.

OEDIPUS
What was thy business? how wast thou employed?

HERDSMAN
The best part of my life I tended sheep.

OEDIPUS
What were the pastures thou didst most frequent?

HERDSMAN
Cithaeron and the neighboring alps.   *1 1220*

OEDIPUS
                        Then there
Thou must have known yon man, at least by fame?

HERDSMAN
Yon man? in what way? what man dost thou mean?

OEDIPUS
The man here, having met him in past times...

HERDSMAN
Off-hand I cannot call him well to mind.

MESSENGER
No wonder, master. But I will revive
His blunted memories. Sure he can recall
What time together both we drove our flocks,
He two, I one, on the Cithaeron range,
For three long summers; I his mate from spring   *l↙ 30*
Till rose Arcturus; then in winter time
I led mine home, he his to Laius' folds.
Did these things happen as I say, or no?

HERDSMAN
'Tis long ago, but all thou say'st is true.

MESSENGER
Well, thou mast then remember giving me
A child to rear as my own foster-son?

HERDSMAN
Why dost thou ask this question? What of that?

MESSENGER
Friend, he that stands before thee was that child.

HERDSMAN
A plague upon thee! Hold thy wanton tongue!

OEDIPUS
Softly, old man, rebuke him not; thy words   *1 2↗40*
Are more deserving chastisement than his.

HERDSMAN
O best of masters, what is my offense?

OEDIPUS
Not answering what he asks about the child.

HERDSMAN
He speaks at random, babbles like a fool.

OEDIPUS
If thou lack'st grace to speak, I'll loose thy tongue.

HERDSMAN
For mercy's sake abuse not an old man.

OEDIPUS
Arrest the villain, seize and pinion him!

HERDSMAN
Alack, alack!
What have I done? what wouldst thou further learn?

OEDIPUS
Didst give this man the child of whom he asks?   , 250

HERDSMAN
I did; and would that I had died that day!

OEDIPUS
And die thou shalt unless thou tell the truth.

HERDSMAN
But, if I tell it, I am doubly lost.

OEDIPUS
The knave methinks will still prevaricate.

HERDSMAN
Nay, I confessed I gave it long ago.

OEDIPUS
Whence came it? was it thine, or given to thee?

HERDSMAN
I had it from another, 'twas not mine.

OEDIPUS
From whom of these our townsmen, and what house?

HERDSMAN
Forbear for God's sake, master, ask no more.

OEDIPUS
If I must question thee again, thou'rt lost.   I 260

HERDSMAN
Well then—it was a child of Laius' house.

OEDIPUS
Slave-born or one of Laius' own race?

HERDSMAN
Ah me!
I stand upon the perilous edge of speech.

OEDIPUS
And I of hearing, but I still must hear.

HERDSMAN
Know then the child was by repute his own,
But she within, thy consort best could tell.

OEDIPUS
What! she, she gave it thee?

HERDSMAN
                'Tis so, my king.

OEDIPUS
With what intent?

HERDSMAN
                To make away with it.   1280

OEDIPUS
What, she its mother.

HERDSMAN
                Fearing a dread weird.

OEDIPUS
What weird?

HERDSMAN
                'Twas told that he should slay his sire.

OEDIPUS
What didst thou give it then to this old man?

HERDSMAN

Through pity, master, for the babe. I thought
He'd take it to the country whence he came;
But he preserved it for the worst of woes.
For if thou art in sooth what this man saith,
God pity thee! thou wast to misery born.   l 260

OEDIPUS

Ah me! ah me! all brought to pass, all true!
O light, may I behold thee nevermore!
I stand a wretch, in birth, in wedlock cursed,
A parricide, incestuously, triply cursed!
[Exit OEDIPUS]

CHORUS
(Str. 1)
          Races of mortal man
          Whose life is but a span,
I count ye but the shadow of a shade!
          For he who most doth know
          Of bliss, hath but the show;
A moment, and the visions pale and fade.   l 290
Thy fall, O Oedipus, thy piteous fall
Warns me none born of women blest to call.

(Ant. 1)
          For he of marksmen best,
          O Zeus, outshot the rest,
And won the prize supreme of wealth and power.
          By him the vulture maid
          Was quelled, her witchery laid;
He rose our savior and the land's strong tower.
We hailed thee king and from that day adored
Of mighty Thebes the universal lord.   l 300

(Str. 2)
          O heavy hand of fate!
          Who now more desolate,
Whose tale more sad than thine, whose lot more dire?
          O Oedipus, discrowned head,
          Thy cradle was thy marriage bed;
One harborage sufficed for son and sire.

How could the soil thy father eared so long
Endure to bear in silence such a wrong?

(Ant. 2)
    All-seeing Time hath caught
    Guilt, and to justice brought   (3 (0
The son and sire commingled in one bed.
    O child of Laius' ill-starred race
    Would I had ne'er beheld thy face;
I raise for thee a dirge as o'er the dead.
Yet, sooth to say, through thee I drew new breath,
And now through thee I feel a second death.
[Enter SECOND MESSENGER.]

SECOND MESSENGER
Most grave and reverend senators of Thebes,
What Deeds ye soon must hear, what sights behold
How will ye mourn, if, true-born patriots,
Ye reverence still the race of Labdacus!   (3 2-0
Not Ister nor all Phasis' flood, I ween,
Could wash away the blood-stains from this house,
The ills it shrouds or soon will bring to light,
Ills wrought of malice, not unwittingly.
The worst to bear are self-inflicted wounds.

CHORUS
Grievous enough for all our tears and groans
Our past calamities; what canst thou add?

SECOND MESSENGER
My tale is quickly told and quickly heard.
Our sovereign lady queen Jocasta's dead.

CHORUS
Alas, poor queen! how came she by her death?   1/3 3 0

SECOND MESSENGER
By her own hand. And all the horror of it,
Not having seen, yet cannot comprehend.
Nathless, as far as my poor memory serves,
I will relate the unhappy lady's woe.
When in her frenzy she had passed inside
The vestibule, she hurried straight to win

The bridal-chamber, clutching at her hair
With both her hands, and, once within the room,
She shut the doors behind her with a crash.
"Laius," she cried, and called her husband dead   l 3 40
Long, long ago; her thought was of that child
By him begot, the son by whom the sire
Was murdered and the mother left to breed
With her own seed, a monstrous progeny.
Then she bewailed the marriage bed whereon
Poor wretch, she had conceived a double brood,
Husband by husband, children by her child.
What happened after that I cannot tell,
Nor how the end befell, for with a shriek
Burst on us Oedipus; all eyes were fixed   l 350
On Oedipus, as up and down he strode,
Nor could we mark her agony to the end.
For stalking to and fro "A sword!" he cried,
"Where is the wife, no wife, the teeming womb
That bore a double harvest, me and mine?"
And in his frenzy some supernal power
(No mortal, surely, none of us who watched him)
Guided his footsteps; with a terrible shriek,
As though one beckoned him, he crashed against
The folding doors, and from their staples forced   l 360
The wrenched bolts and hurled himself within.
Then we beheld the woman hanging there,
A running noose entwined about her neck.
But when he saw her, with a maddened roar
He loosed the cord; and when her wretched corpse
Lay stretched on earth, what followed—O 'twas dread!
He tore the golden brooches that upheld
Her queenly robes, upraised them high and smote
Full on his eye-balls, uttering words like these:
"No more shall ye behold such sights of woe,   l 370
Deeds I have suffered and myself have wrought;
Henceforward quenched in darkness shall ye see
Those ye should ne'er have seen; now blind to those
Whom, when I saw, I vainly yearned to know."
    Such was the burden of his moan, whereto,
Not once but oft, he struck with his hand uplift
His eyes, and at each stroke the ensanguined orbs
Bedewed his beard, not oozing drop by drop,
But one black gory downpour, thick as hail.

Such evils, issuing from the double source,   1380
Have whelmed them both, confounding man and wife.
Till now the storied fortune of this house
Was fortunate indeed; but from this day
Woe, lamentation, ruin, death, disgrace,
All ills that can be named, all, all are theirs.

CHORUS
But hath he still no respite from his pain?

SECOND MESSENGER
He cries, "Unbar the doors and let all Thebes
Behold the slayer of his sire, his mother's—"
That shameful word my lips may not repeat.
He vows to fly self-banished from the land,   1390
Nor stay to bring upon his house the curse
Himself had uttered; but he has no strength
Nor one to guide him, and his torture's more
Than man can suffer, as yourselves will see.
For lo, the palace portals are unbarred,
And soon ye shall behold a sight so sad
That he who must abhorred would pity it.
[Enter OEDIPUS blinded.]

CHORUS
    Woeful sight! more woeful none
    These sad eyes have looked upon.
    Whence this madness? None can tell   1400
    Who did cast on thee his spell,
    prowling all thy life around,
    Leaping with a demon bound.
    Hapless wretch! how can I brook
    On thy misery to look?
    Though to gaze on thee I yearn,
    Much to question, much to learn,
    Horror-struck away I turn.

OEDIPUS
Ah me! ah woe is me!
Ah whither am I borne!   1410
How like a ghost forlorn
My voice flits from me on the air!
On, on the demon goads. The end, ah where?

CHORUS
An end too dread to tell, too dark to see.

OEDIPUS
(Str. 1)
Dark, dark! The horror of darkness, like a shroud,
Wraps me and bears me on through mist and cloud.
Ah me, ah me! What spasms athwart me shoot,
What pangs of agonizing memory?

CHORUS
No marvel if in such a plight thou feel'st
The double weight of past and present woes.   l 420

OEDIPUS
(Ant. 1)
Ah friend, still loyal, constant still and kind,
        Thou carest for the blind.
I know thee near, and though bereft of eyes,
        Thy voice I recognize.

CHORUS
O doer of dread deeds, how couldst thou mar
Thy vision thus? What demon goaded thee?

OEDIPUS
(Str. 2)
Apollo, friend, Apollo, he it was
        That brought these ills to pass;
But the right hand that dealt the blow
        Was mine, none other. How,   l 430
How, could I longer see when sight
        Brought no delight?

CHORUS
Alas! 'tis as thou sayest.

OEDIPUS
Say, friends, can any look or voice
Or touch of love henceforth my heart rejoice?
        Haste, friends, no fond delay,
        Take the twice cursed away

Far from all ken,
The man abhorred of gods, accursed of men.

CHORUS
O thy despair well suits thy desperate case.　　1440
Would I had never looked upon thy face!

OEDIPUS
(Ant. 2)
My curse on him whoe'er unrived
The waif's fell fetters and my life revived!
He meant me well, yet had he left me there,
He had saved my friends and me a world of care.

CHORUS
I too had wished it so.

OEDIPUS
Then had I never come to shed
My father's blood nor climbed my mother's bed;
The monstrous offspring of a womb defiled,
Co-mate of him who gendered me, and child.　　1450
Was ever man before afflicted thus,
Like Oedipus.

CHORUS
I cannot say that thou hast counseled well,
For thou wert better dead than living blind.

OEDIPUS
What's done was well done. Thou canst never shake
My firm belief. A truce to argument.
For, had I sight, I know not with what eyes
I could have met my father in the shades,
Or my poor mother, since against the twain
I sinned, a sin no gallows could atone.
Aye, but, ye say, the sight of children joys　　1460
A parent's eyes. What, born as mine were born?
No, such a sight could never bring me joy;
Nor this fair city with its battlements,
Its temples and the statues of its gods,
Sights from which I, now wretchedst of all,
Once ranked the foremost Theban in all Thebes,

By my own sentence am cut off, condemned
By my own proclamation 'gainst the wretch,
The miscreant by heaven itself declared
Unclean—and of the race of Laius.   1470
Thus branded as a felon by myself,
How had I dared to look you in the face?
Nay, had I known a way to choke the springs
Of hearing, I had never shrunk to make
A dungeon of this miserable frame,
Cut off from sight and hearing; for 'tis bliss
to bide in regions sorrow cannot reach.
Why didst thou harbor me, Cithaeron, why
Didst thou not take and slay me? Then I never
Had shown to men the secret of my birth.   1480
O Polybus, O Corinth, O my home,
Home of my ancestors (so wast thou called)
How fair a nursling then I seemed, how foul
The canker that lay festering in the bud!
Now is the blight revealed of root and fruit.
Ye triple high-roads, and thou hidden glen,
Coppice, and pass where meet the three-branched ways,
Ye drank my blood, the life-blood these hands spilt,
My father's; do ye call to mind perchance
Those deeds of mine ye witnessed and the work   1490
I wrought thereafter when I came to Thebes?
O fatal wedlock, thou didst give me birth,
And, having borne me, sowed again my seed,
Mingling the blood of fathers, brothers, children,
Brides, wives and mothers, an incestuous brood,
All horrors that are wrought beneath the sun,
Horrors so foul to name them were unmeet.
O, I adjure you, hide me anywhere
Far from this land, or slay me straight, or cast me
Down to the depths of ocean out of sight.   1500
Come hither, deign to touch an abject wretch;
Draw near and fear not; I myself must bear
The load of guilt that none but I can share.
[Enter CREON.]

CREON
Lo, here is Creon, the one man to grant
Thy prayer by action or advice, for he
Is left the State's sole guardian in thy stead.

OEDIPUS

Ah me! what words to accost him can I find?
What cause has he to trust me? In the past
I have bee proved his rancorous enemy.   150

CREON

Not in derision, Oedipus, I come
Nor to upbraid thee with thy past misdeeds.
(To BYSTANDERS)
But shame upon you! if ye feel no sense
Of human decencies, at least revere
The Sun whose light beholds and nurtures all.
Leave not thus nakedly for all to gaze at
A horror neither earth nor rain from heaven
Nor light will suffer. Lead him straight within,
For it is seemly that a kinsman's woes
Be heard by kin and seen by kin alone.

OEDIPUS

O listen, since thy presence comes to me
A shock of glad surprise—so noble thou,
And I so vile—O grant me one small boon.
I ask it not on my behalf, but thine.

CREON

And what the favor thou wouldst crave of me?

OEDIPUS

Forth from thy borders thrust me with all speed;
Set me within some vasty desert where
No mortal voice shall greet me any more.

CREON

This had I done already, but I deemed
It first behooved me to consult the god.

OEDIPUS

His will was set forth fully—to destroy
The parricide, the scoundrel; and I am he.

CREON

Yea, so he spake, but in our present plight

'Twere better to consult the god anew.

OEDIPUS
Dare ye inquire concerning such a wretch?

CREON
Yea, for thyself wouldst credit now his word.

OEDIPUS
Aye, and on thee in all humility
I lay this charge: let her who lies within
Receive such burial as thou shalt ordain;
Such rites 'tis thine, as brother, to perform.
But for myself, O never let my Thebes,
The city of my sires, be doomed to bear
The burden of my presence while I live.
No, let me be a dweller on the hills,
On yonder mount Cithaeron, famed as mine,
My tomb predestined for me by my sire
And mother, while they lived, that I may die
Slain as they sought to slay me, when alive.
This much I know full surely, nor disease
Shall end my days, nor any common chance;
For I had ne'er been snatched from death, unless
I was predestined to some awful doom.
    So be it. I reck not how Fate deals with me
But my unhappy children—for my sons
Be not concerned, O Creon, they are men,
And for themselves, where'er they be, can fend.
But for my daughters twain, poor innocent maids,
Who ever sat beside me at the board
Sharing my viands, drinking of my cup,
For them, I pray thee, care, and, if thou willst,
O might I feel their touch and make my moan.
Hear me, O prince, my noble-hearted prince!
Could I but blindly touch them with my hands
I'd think they still were mine, as when I saw.
[ANTIGONE and ISMENE are led in.]
What say I? can it be my pretty ones
Whose sobs I hear? Has Creon pitied me
And sent me my two darlings? Can this be?

CREON

'Tis true; 'twas I procured thee this delight,
Knowing the joy they were to thee of old.

OEDIPUS
God speed thee! and as meed for bringing them
May Providence deal with thee kindlier
Than it has dealt with me! O children mine,
Where are ye? Let me clasp you with these hands,
A brother's hands, a father's; hands that made
Lack-luster sockets of his once bright eyes;
Hands of a man who blindly, recklessly,
Became your sire by her from whom he sprang.
Though I cannot behold you, I must weep
In thinking of the evil days to come,
The slights and wrongs that men will put upon you.
Where'er ye go to feast or festival,
No merrymaking will it prove for you,
But oft abashed in tears ye will return.
And when ye come to marriageable years,
Where's the bold wooers who will jeopardize
To take unto himself such disrepute
As to my children's children still must cling,
For what of infamy is lacking here?
"Their father slew his father, sowed the seed
Where he himself was gendered, and begat
These maidens at the source wherefrom he sprang."
Such are the gibes that men will cast at you.
Who then will wed you? None, I ween, but ye
Must pine, poor maids, in single barrenness.
O Prince, Menoeceus' son, to thee, I turn,
With the it rests to father them, for we
Their natural parents, both of us, are lost.
O leave them not to wander poor, unwed,
Thy kin, nor let them share my low estate.
O pity them so young, and but for thee
All destitute. Thy hand upon it, Prince.
To you, my children I had much to say,
Were ye but ripe to hear. Let this suffice:
Pray ye may find some home and live content,
And may your lot prove happier than your sire's.

CREON
Thou hast had enough of weeping; pass within.

OEDIPUS

                        I must obey,

Though 'tis grievous.

CREON

             Weep not, everything must have its day.

OEDIPUS

Well I go, but on conditions.

CREON

                What thy terms for going, say.

OEDIPUS

Send me from the land an exile.

CREON

                Ask this of the gods, not me.

OEDIPUS

But I am the gods' abhorrence.

CREON

                  Then they soon will grant thy plea.

OEDIPUS

Lead me hence, then, I am willing.

CREON

                  Come, but let thy children go.

OEDIPUS

Rob me not of these my children!

CREON

                Crave not mastery in all,

For the mastery that raised thee was thy bane and wrought thy fall.

CHORUS

Look ye, countrymen and Thebans, this is Oedipus the great,
He who knew the Sphinx's riddle and was mightiest in our state.

Who of all our townsmen gazed not on his fame with envious eyes?
Now, in what a sea of troubles sunk and overwhelmed he lies!
Therefore wait to see life's ending ere thou count one mortal blest;
Wait till free from pain and sorrow he has gained his final rest.

Made in the USA
Columbia, SC
20 January 2021